Purpose: The purpose of this book is to provide basic reading for children ages 1 and up. Please feel free to contact me at littleyapperbooks@gmail.com for comments.

About the author: Jane is an author, designer and educator. These days, you will find her drawing and writing children's books. She draws her inspiration from her students and her children. Jane lives in the Big Apple with her husband, two children and beloved yorkies.

Author Page: www.amazon.com/author/janethai

Author's Notes

Help your child begin and build their first words in Chinese. This easy to follow picture word book is written in both English and simplified Chinese. Children learn best with visuals and can be taught to be bilingual at a very young age. In fact, it is recommended that they learn another language as early as possible. This book contains many everyday objects in a home that children will see. Help your child reinforce vocabulary by pointing to real life objects at home or anywhere else.
If you do not speak Chinese, you can still teach your child and give them a starting foundation to work with. Audio files of this book can be downloaded free with purchase of the book at littleyapper.com. Have fun learning together!

Learn more about how to teach your child a second language at littleyapper.com.

LIVE & LEARN

I belong to:

Intro:

The Chinese character 家(jiā) consists of two radicals. 宀 (mián) and 豕(shǐ). 宀 is the radical for roof. 豕 is both a radical and a character that means pig or swine. Together 家 (jiā) means home, house and family.

A pig under the roof represents a household asset of a family. During the beginning of the agricultural era in China, many households raised pigs. It was an asset that a family could sell, trade or use as food. Pigs were domesticated and lived in homes, therefore, the character of the pig under the roof became the character for home.

HOME

家
jiā

bathroom
浴室
yùshì
dining room
饭厅
fàntīng
living room
客厅
kètīng

bedroom
卧室
wòshì
Rooms
房间
fángjiān
厨房
chúfáng
kitchen
车库
chēkù
garage

地毯
dìtǎn
rug

newspaper
报纸
bàozhǐ

Living Room

display case
陈列柜
chénliè guì

throw pillow

靠枕
kàozhěn

客厅

kètīng

book shelf

书架

shūjià

画

huà

painting

television

电视

diànshì

end table

茶几

chájī

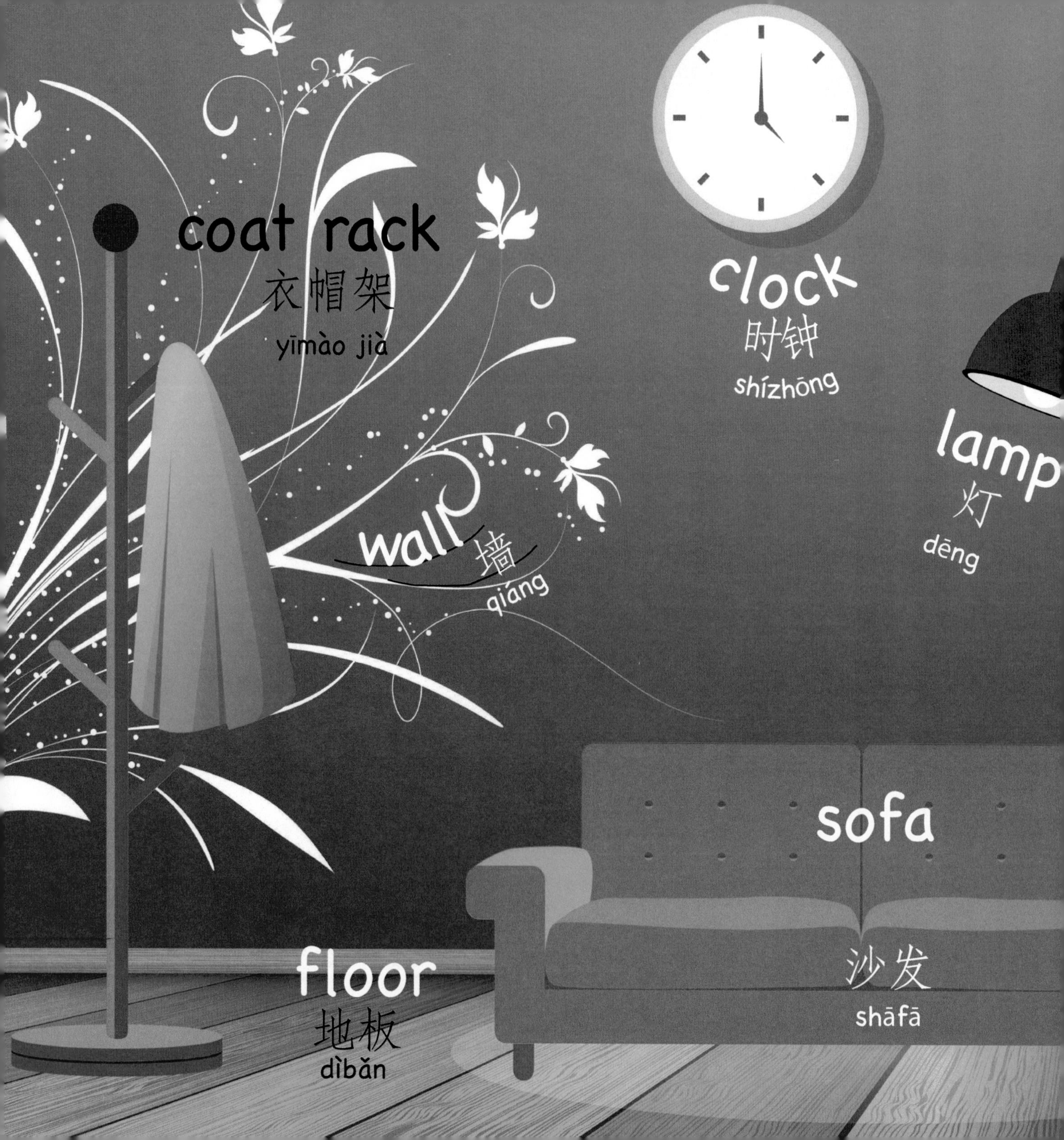
coat rack
衣帽架
yīmào jià
clock
时钟
shízhōng
lamp
灯
dēng
wall
墙
qiáng
sofa
沙发
shāfā
floor
地板
dìbǎn

curtains

窗帘

chuānglián

window

窗户

chuānghù

咖啡桌

kāfēi zhuō

coffee table

毛刷
máoshuā
hairbrush

Bath Room

towel
毛巾
máojīn

bathtube
浴缸
yùgāng

toilet paper

卫生纸
wèishēng zhǐ

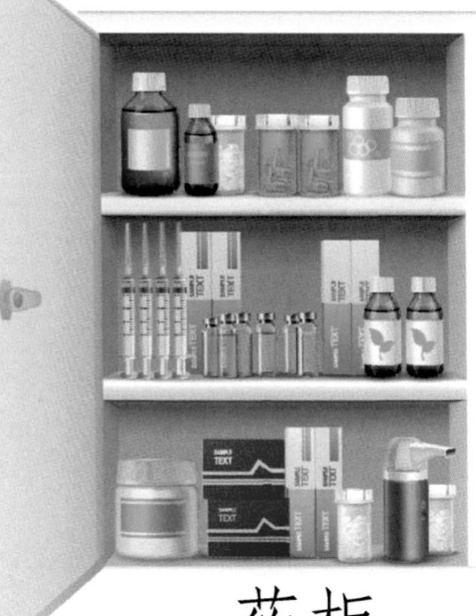

medicine cabinet

药柜
yàoguì

toilet

厕所
cèsuǒ

sink

洗手槽
xǐshǒu cáo

rubber ducky

橡皮鸭

xiàngpí yā

comb

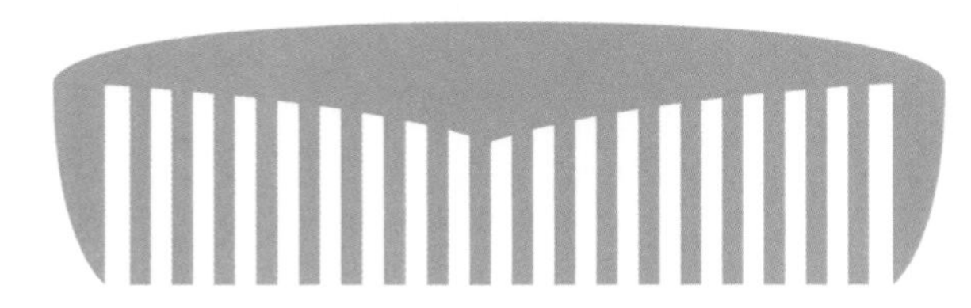

梳子

shūzi

toothbrush

牙刷

yáshuā

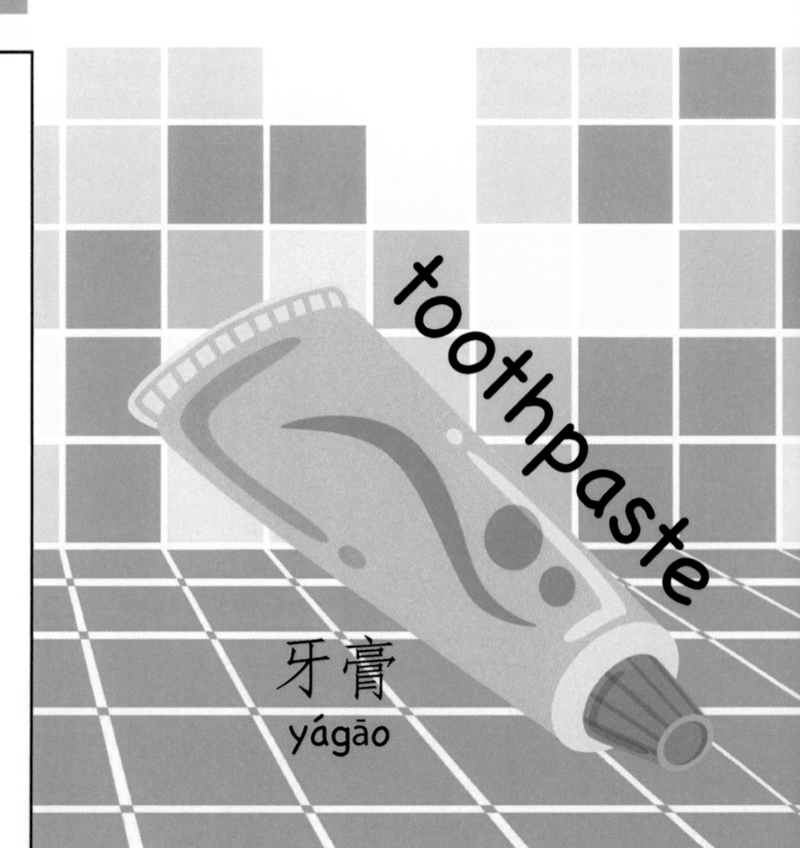

toothpaste

牙膏

yágāo

吹风机

chuīfēng jī

hair dryer

洗发水

xǐfǎ shuǐ

SHAMPOO

肥皂

féizào

护发素

hùfǎ sù

fork

叉子

chāzi

knife

刀子

dāozi

Dining Room

杯子

bēizi

cup

桌子

zhuōzi

table

饭厅
fàntīng

spoon
调羹
tiáogēng

napkin
餐巾
cānjīn

chair
椅子
yǐzi

plate
盘子
pánzi

breakfast

早餐

zǎocān

lunch

午餐

wǔcān

fried rice

炒饭 chǎofàn

pork soup dumplings

小笼包 xiǎo lóng bāo

dinner
晚餐
wǎncān

甜点
tiándiǎn
dessert

筷子
kuàizi
chopsticks

bowl
碗
wǎn

Kitchen

frying pan

平底锅

píngdǐ guō

spatula

锅铲

guōchǎn

stir spoon

搅拌勺

jiǎobàn sháo

glove

手套

shǒutào

pot 汤锅
tāngguō

厨房
chúfáng

cutting board

Exhaust fan

抽油烟机

chōuyóu yānjī

cupboard

橱柜

chúguì

gas stove

dish washer

煤气炉

méiqì lú

洗碗机

xǐwǎn jī

microwave

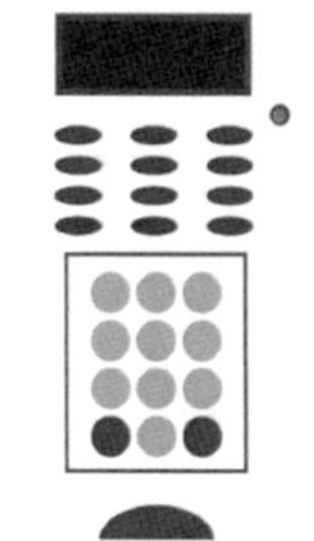

微波炉

wéibō lú

toaster

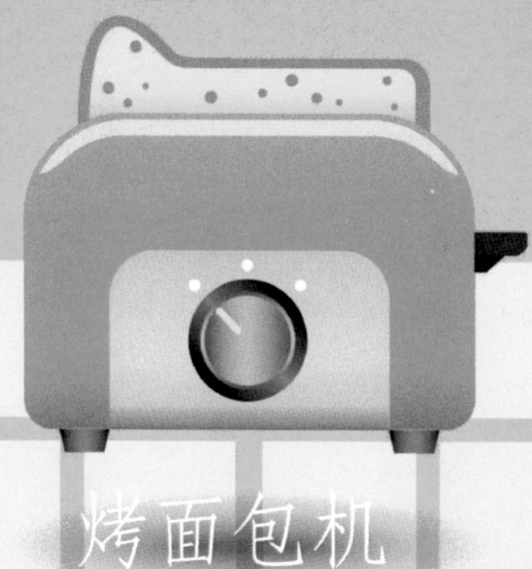

烤面包机

kǎo miànbāo jī

refrigerator

冰箱

bīngxiāng

garbage can

垃圾桶

lèsè tǒng

slippers

拖鞋 tuōxié

blanket

毯子
tǎnzi

bedroom

pillow

枕头
zhěntou

toy bear

玩具熊
wánjù xióng

卧室

wòshì

table lamp

台灯

táidēng

books

书

shū

pajamas

睡衣

shuìyī

梳妆台

shūzhuāngtái

dresser

computer

电脑
diànnǎo

photograph

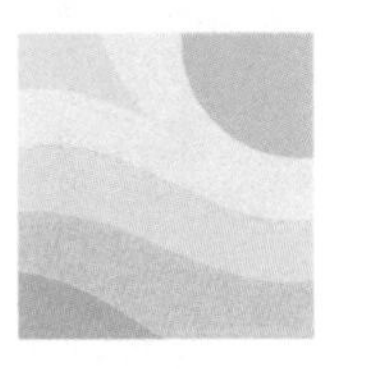

照片
zhàopiàn

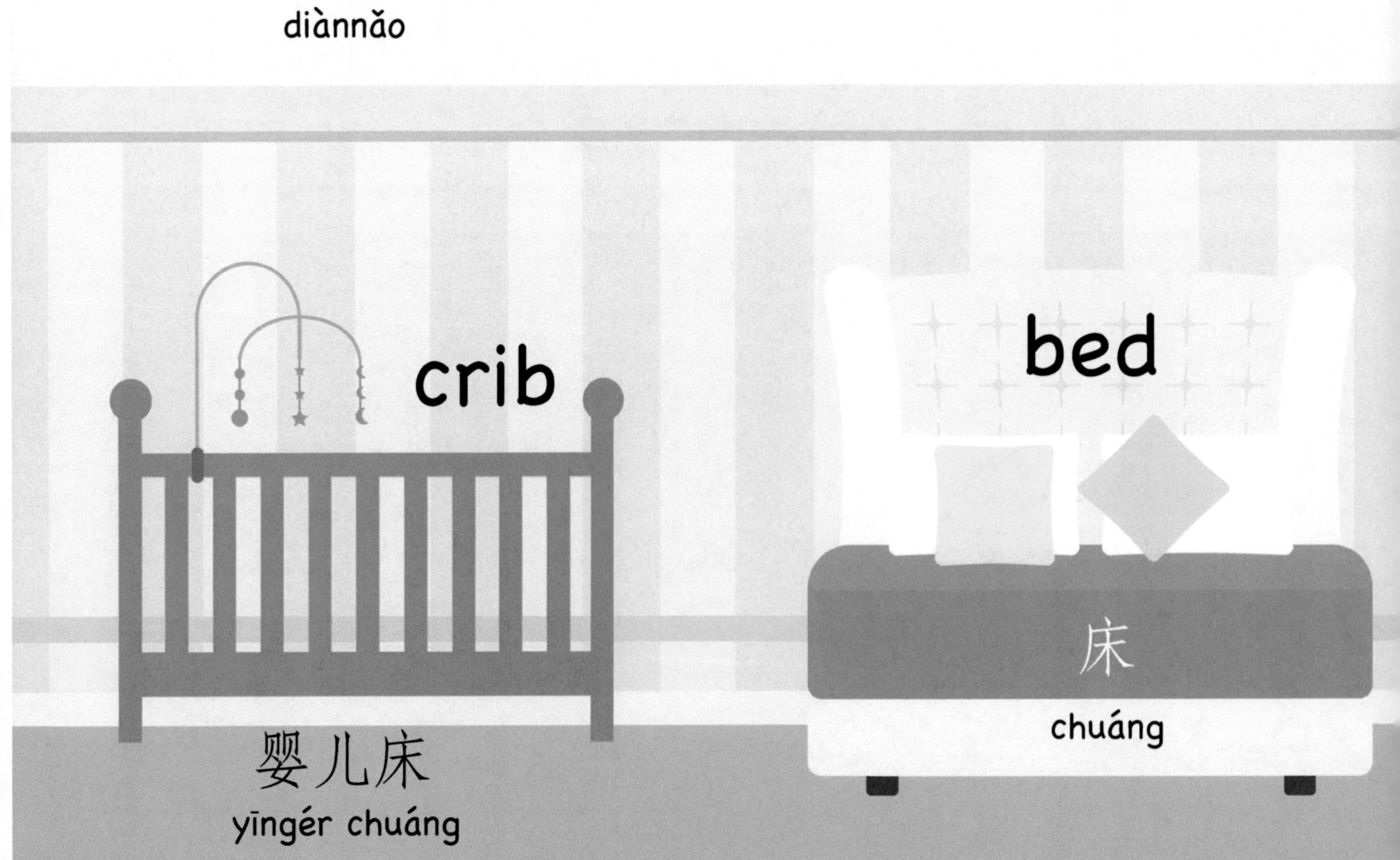

clothes
衣服
yīfú

alarm clock
闹钟
nàozhōng

drawer
抽屉
chōutì

wardrobe
衣柜
yīguì

盒子

hézi

garage

mop

拖把

tuōbǎ

自行车

zìxíngchē

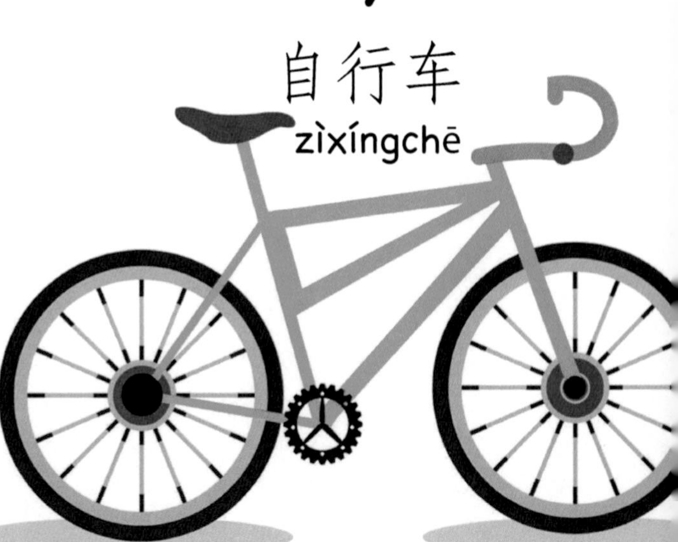

sponge

海绵

hǎimián

垃圾铲

lèsè chǎn

dust pan

车库

chēkù

清洁用品

qīngjié yòngpǐn

cleaning products

broom

扫帚

sàozhǒu

SPIDER
WEB
蜘蛛网
zhīzhū wǎng

laundry basket
洗衣篮
xǐyī lán

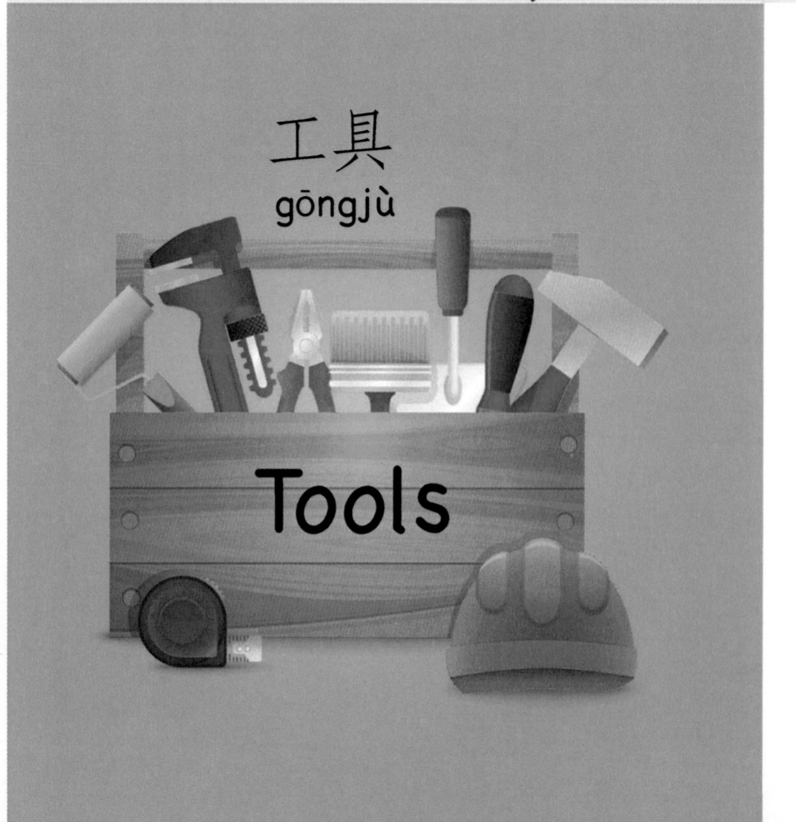
工具
gōngjù
Tools

laundry
detergent
洗衣粉
xǐyī fěn

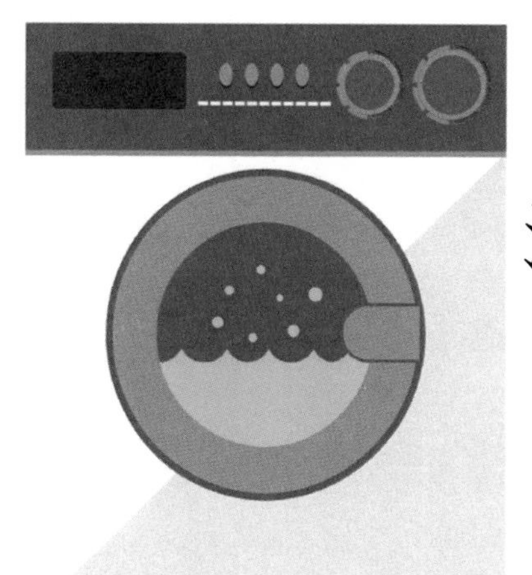

洗衣机

xǐyī jī

washing machine

Ironing board

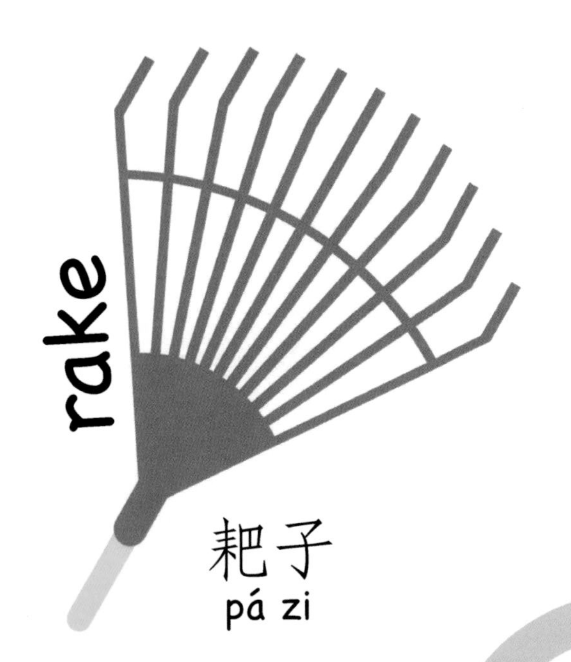

rake

耙子

pá zi

garden shears

园林剪

yuánlín jiǎn

garden

靴子

xuēzi

boots

garden gloves

园丁手套

yuándīng shǒutà

花园

huāyuán

watering can

浇水壶

jiāoshuǐ hú

water hose

水管 shuǐguǎn

plant

植物

zhíwù

园丁叉

yuándīng chā

garden fork

hand trowel

手铲

shǒuchǎn

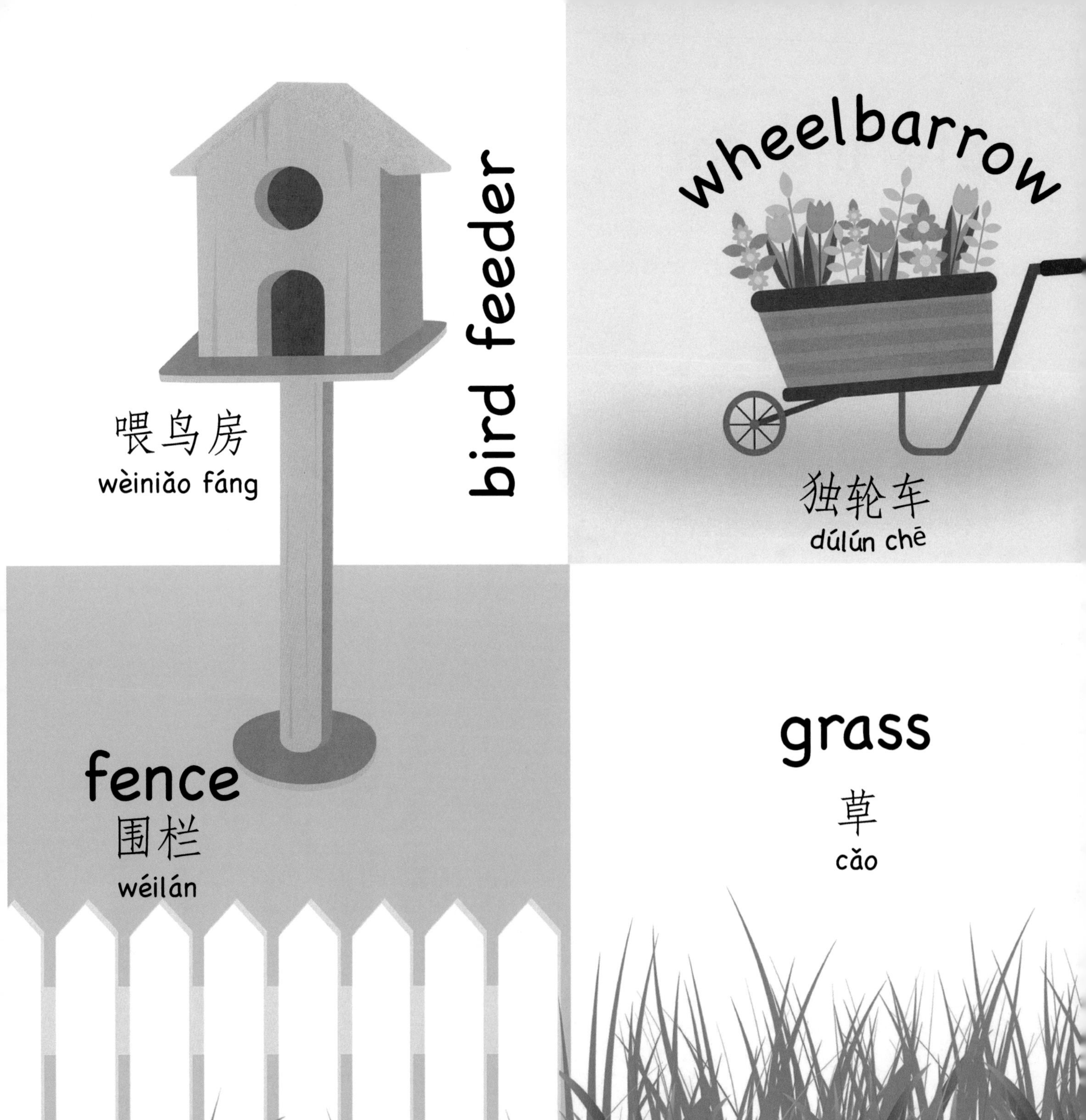
bird feeder
喂鸟房
wèiniǎo fáng
wheelbarrow
独轮车
dúlún chē
fence
围栏
wéilán
grass
草
cǎo

ladybug

瓢虫

piáochóng

shovel

铲子

chǎnzi

flowers

花

huā

vegetables

蔬菜

shūcài

Family

家庭

jiātíng

mother 妈妈

māma

哥哥

gēge

big brother

弟弟

dìdi

little brother

father 爸爸
bàba

baby 宝宝
bǎobao
姐姐
jiějie
big sister

妹妹
mèimei
little sister

maternal
grandfather

外婆 wàipó

maternal
grandmother

mother's
parents

māma de fùmǔ

爷爷 yéye

paternal grandfather

奶奶 nǎinai

paternal grandmother

爸爸的父母
bàba de fùmǔ

father's parents

宠物
chǒngwù

故事结束

gùshì jiéshù

If you have enjoyed this book, please share and leave me a comment at **littleyapper.com**. A review on Amazon.com would be appreciated as well. Thank you. 谢谢

Use code : **FIRSTWORDS** to download your FREE audio book and find out more tips on dual language learning at **littleyapper.com**

Other dual language books by Jane Thai

The Apple Tree
How the World got its Color from the Sea
12 Months of the Year
How Mommy Carries Her Baby
I like Pickles
First Words in Chinese

Made in the USA
Las Vegas, NV
05 May 2021